Maxie's Magnificent Adventures

Volume 1

Ed Larson

ISBN: Softcover   978-1-7960-1442-6
        Hardcover   978-1-7960-1443-3
        EBook   978-1-7960-1441-9

Print information available on the last page

Rev. date: 02/28/2019

To order additional copies of this book, contact:
Xlibris
1-888-795-4274
www.Xlibris.com
Orders@Xlibris.com

Foreword

On Friday May 4th, 2018 our precious dog Maxie passed away in our arms at the age of 14. This book is dedicated to her memory. She will retain a special place in our hearts forever. She was a marvelous companion and brought joy to many with her friendly demeanor and a tail that seemed to be constantly wagging.

Maxie was the centerpiece of a number of my writings and poems. This book contains the "Maxie's Magnificent Adventures" series. These stories were written over a number of years with our growing Grandchildren being the subject of these "Adventures". The "Epilogue" was written shortly after Maxie's passing and read to the family at her memorial service. My wish is that you and yours enjoy this book and, through it, keep your memories of your "Maxies" alive. Sharing this book has helped me through the great pain of her loss. She was so much more to me than "Just a dog". Ed

Maxie's Magnificent Adventures
Part 1

Catalina Cruisin'
With
Kira and Macy

On a pleasant weekend last spring, Kira and Macy went to visit their grandparents, Nana and Papa Ed, at their home in Laguna Beach. It was to be a sleepover. Their parents, Rory and Jaynee, dropped them off just before noon on Saturday. The girls hadn't had their lunch yet because Nana had planned one of her famous picnic lunches for them and they wanted to have a good appetite for that. Upon arrival, they saw that Nana and Papa Ed had already loaded up the car and Maxie, their English Cocker, was anxiously waiting for them in the back seat. She loved it when the girls came to visit, especially sleepovers. Kira and Macy hopped in, gave Maxie hugs and kisses, and off they all went up the hill to Moulton Meadows Park for their picnic.

At the Park, they picked out a nice picnic bench just up the grassy hill from the basketball courts and playground. The playground had lots of fun things to play on so the girls ran down the hill and over to their favorite apparatus. Macy went straight to the mini-merry-go-round that you can make spin around and go faster and faster as you pull yourself to the center post. She was an expert at this and would go through a very impressive acrobatic routine as she spun around. Other kids would stop and admire her talent. Papa Ed had tried it once but got so dizzy that he couldn't walk straight and has never tried it again.

Meanwhile, Kira was climbing on the rope maze that was strung between tall poles that were spread across the sand covered play ground. She was very good too and could climb from one side to the other without ever having to touch the sand which she pretended was hot lava just to make it a little more exciting.

Fun at the park

Up on the hill, Nana started unpacking the picnic basket while Papa Ed tossed the Frisbee to Maxie. Maxie absolutely loved chasing the Frisbee but every once in a while she would wander down and pay a visit to Kira and Macy. But dogs aren't allowed to go on the playground sand so after a brief hello she went back to work punishing that beat up old Frisbee.

Moulton Meadows is a beautiful park that sits high above the ocean and about a mile from the beach. It borders a large wilderness area lined with deep canyons and high rocky ridges that are crisscrossed with narrow hiking trails. Deer, coyotes, and rabbits are abundant in the area and hikers need to also be on the lookout for rattlesnakes. Nana often hikes the trails during the week with Maxie and loves to take pictures of the many wildflowers she finds along the way. Springtime is especially colorful as the hillsides are covered with clusters of golden Monkey Flower and lining the trails can be found purple Mariposa Lilies, lavender Night Shade, and crimson Indian Paint Brush. Nana has educated Papa Ed about wildflowers over the years and he often joins Nana on the weekend hikes. He gets excited when he finds a new wildflower that Nana can't identify.

The girls were getting pretty hungry so they decided to go see how

Nana was coming with lunch preparation. Nana said it would be another 10 minutes or so. It was at that moment that Maxie decided to head off into the wilderness area in hot pursuit of a rabbit she had spooked. The girls went running off down the trail after her. They were only a little ways down the trail when they heard Maxie let out a long string of barks further down the trail. They kept on running in that direction to see what all the excitement was about.

It had been a year or so earlier that Kira and Macy had been hiking this same trail with Papa Ed when he showed them a very special little spot. Just to the side of the trail was a narrow tunnel through the underbrush that led to a shady chamber that was formed by a bunch of overhanging branches from a thicket of scrub oaks. The tunnel was barely big enough for Papa Ed to get through if he crawled on all fours. Inside the chamber there were low running thick oak branches that made perfect benches. There had even been a little swing that someone had hung from the overhead branches. The chamber couldn't be seen from the trail and Papa Ed had called it "The Secret Place". They always stopped at "The Secret Place" when they hiked this trail and the only others Papa Ed had ever told about "The Secret Place" were Nana and the girls' two cousins Evan and Grayson.

Still in hot pursuit of Maxie, the girls had run all the way to "The Secret Place" and were about to pass by it when they heard something strange coming from within. That scared them both and they started to high tail it back up the trail when they heard what sounded like their names being called out, but it sounded different from what they were used to. It wasn't "Ki-ra" but instead it was "Krrrrrrrrr- Ah" and instead of "Ma-cy" it was "Maaaaaaa-Cy". This made them curious enough to overcome their fear and they slowly turned and walked back to the entrance of "The Secret Place". Kira knelt down and peered into the shadows of the chamber. She quickly turned and said to Macy, "You're not going to believe this! Take a look". When Macy looked inside, she saw Maxie sitting up on a branch with a big smile on her face and was shocked when she heard Maxie say, "Come on in girls, it's time for you to have your first great adventure with me". Macy stumbled backwards out of the entrance and fell right on her butt. She stared up wide eyed into the face of her sister, "Did you just hear what I heard Sissy?" and was very relieved when Kira, with her mouth open wide in amazement, slowly nodded that she had heard it too.

Trembling with excitement, and maybe some fear, the girls slowly crawled into The Secret Place. It had always been a little dark and sometimes a bit cool in The Secret Place but now they noticed that it was even darker than usual and almost cold. Once they were inside they stood up with their hands on their hips and faced Maxie. "You almost scared the skin off us Maxie" scolded Kira. "What's the big idea?" "Yah" said Macy, "and I got my shorts all dirty when I fell on my butt out there". "Get a grip girls." replied Maxie, "You're in for a real exciting afternoon. Now just follow me!" and she scampered to the back corner of The Secret Place. Maxie shouted "Geronimo" and disappeared down a small hole that the girls had never noticed before.

Kira shouted "No don't Maxie!" and ran over to the hole, but Maxie was long gone. Kira looked over at Macy and asked, "Now what do we do?" Macy said, "You heard what Maxie said, let's go" and she dove headfirst down the hole. Kira wasn't so sure that was the right decision but there was no way that she was going to let her sister go off on an adventure by herself so she softly said "Geronimo. I hope." and slid feet first down the dark hole. Down and down they went, winding through the blackness until finally they saw a bright light at the end of the long tunnel and like two cannon balls they flew out the end of the tunnel and landed with a heavy "thud" on the sandy beach over a mile below Moulton Meadows. "WOW! That was better than anything at Disneyland" exclaimed Macy. "It sure was!" agreed Kira.

They turned toward the ocean and saw that Maxie was waiting for them down at the waters edge. "Come on girls! Let's get going while the tide is just right. No time to waste". They ran over to see Maxie standing on top of a small raft made from wooden logs that had been tied together with some rope. It looked like it might have drifted all the way to California from the Tsunami in Japan. It certainly wasn't very sturdy looking. "Wait a minute Maxie." said Kira. "Before we go any further how about telling us where we're supposed to be going".

With that, Maxie faced out to the open water, stood on three legs and extended her right paw majestically to the West. "We're cruising to Catalina Island girls and it's time we shoved off, so climb on board" she pronounced with authority. Since they had come this far and things had seemed to work out, the girls clamored onto the raft and soon the tide was carrying them out into the ocean. Maxie moved to the rear of the raft and hung her hindquarters over the edge and stuck her wagging tail into the water. They felt the wind in their faces as they quickly started picking up speed. That dog's tail was amazing!

After an hour or so, Maxie pronounced, "My tail needs a break. It's time for some fun" and with that she catapulted off the raft in the direction of a big pelican that was paddling out on the waves. When it came to chasing birds of any kind, Maxie just couldn't help herself. As she sped towards the unconcerned pelican, she was unaware that, in the depths far below, swam a very mean and hungry creature.

Chasing Polly

Draco, the Mako shark, stared upward through the blue water and saw the silhouette of it's soon to be lunch swimming across the water in pursuit of a bird that she would never catch. Draco thought, "It serves that mutt right that it should be a snack for me. She should know by now that there is no way that she can catch that bird yet she keeps right on trying. I guess there must be something about "the joy of the chase". Well, that dog's chasing days are soon to be over", and upward he surged, heading right at Maxie's soft little tummy. Mako sharks aren't as big as the great whites but they are much faster, so Draco reached Maxie in only seconds.

As Maxie swam closer to the pelican, instead of flying away, the bird suddenly turned and said "Maxie, stop fooling around or you just might be somebody's snack". Maxie knew Polly the Pelican quite well because they had played this game many times before. Polly often tried to convince Maxie not to chase her, so Maxie thought this was just another ploy to distract her from her goal of finally catching this wily pelican. Then suddenly she felt an enormous pressure from below and was launched head over heels high into the air. She felt herself starting to fall and twisted to look down and what she saw made her tail stop wagging and her eyes go wide. Below was the biggest jaw and set of razor sharp teeth she had ever seen. Even bigger than those of that big German Sheppard that lived down the street. In that instant she realized it was all over. No more treats, no more tummy rubs, no more Frisbee, and worst of all, no more wonderful play time with Kira, Macy, Evan, and Grayson.

She had resigned herself to her fate when, off to the side, there was an explosion of water and from the center of the explosion came what looked like a sleek gray torpedo. The nose of the torpedo rammed directly into Maxie's side and, although it knocked all the breath right out of her, the blow succeeded in thrusting her clear of Draco's waiting jaws. Just then, two more torpedoes smacked right into either side of Draco and he let out a loud grunt of pain and yelled, "I'm out of here!" and dove quickly into the safety of the deep. Maxie was paddling around trying to catch her breath when Dolly the dolphin surfaced next to her and said "Won't you ever learn to be more careful Maxie? How do you expect to complete your adventure if you become an appetizer?" Maxie looked sheepish and said, "Thanks for saving me Dolly, I'll try to be more careful in the future but I just couldn't help myself when I saw Polly paddling around like she owned the whole ocean."

Saved by Dolly

Maxie then introduced Dolly to Kira and Macy and even asked Polly to come over so she could meet the girls. They were all exchanging pleasantries when Polly made an observation. "Don't look now but this old raft is starting to come apart." Sure enough they looked down and saw that most of the rope holding the raft's logs together was badly frayed and starting to unravel. "This thing is never going to make it to Catalina" said Dolly. Hearing that, Kira and Macy got real worried looks on their faces and turned to Maxie. Kira said, "Well you got us into this mess, now what are you going to do to get us out of it? We're both good swimmers but I don't think we can make it all the way to Catalina from here." Maxie started scratching behind her right ear like she does when she's thinking over complicated things, but she didn't seem to be coming up with any ideas. It was Dolly who said, "I think me and my friends might be able to help". She stuck her head down into the water and let out a long string of squeaky sounds and in a minute the heads of two more dolphins appeared.

It was truly a magnificent sight! Dolly was in the lead with Maxie standing tall and proud on her back. She was flanked by her two dolphin friends with Kira on one and Macy on the other, straddling their backs like they were horses. They were skimming over the waves at incredible speed.

The wind in their hair and the salt spray on their faces was exhilarating. "Oh Baby!!" yelped Maxie. "Awesome!!" yelled Kira. "Watch this!!" shouted Macy and they turned to see her go into a perfect handstand on top of her racing dolphin. Up ahead, Polly was flying low over the water, leading the trio on a straight course to Catalina.

It took very little time to cross the remaining miles and soon they had arrived on the beach at Avalon, the small port village on the East side of Catalina Island. They thanked Polly and Dolly and, with Maxie, headed off to explore the island. Dolly shouted after them, "When you're ready to go back to Laguna Beach, just go out to the point on the south end of the village and have Maxie call for us and we'll come get you. Have fun!" And with that, Dolly and her two friends turned and swam back out into deep water. Polly also circled back and headed east but not before dropping a big bird poop right on the top of Maxie's head. "That's just a reminder that you'll never be able to catch me" she yelled. Maxie, made a valiant effort to jump up and snatch a tail feather but fell far short. "I'll get you for that" she yelled after the retreating pelican and then dove in the water to clean off the mess.

They headed off to explore Avalon and, after passing many little shops and restaurants, they came to a small pier jutting out into the harbor. Tied to the pier was one boat that looked very different from the others. There was a long canopy over the top of the boat and, looking inside the dark interior, they could see rows of benches. Beneath the benches, they were surprised to see that the bottom of the boat was glass. From behind them they heard, "Hi girls, are you interested in a ride in my boat?" They turned to see a tall man with a sea captain's hat and a long gray beard smiling down at them. He had a curved wooden pipe sticking out the side of his mouth and the pleasant smell of tobacco was riding on the breeze.

Kira said to Macy, "I don't have any money with me, do you?" and Macy shook her head no. They both looked at Maxie who was distracted by a seagull that had landed just down the pier. "I'm sure Maxie doesn't have any money either Sissy" said Macy. Overhearing this, the man said "I tell you what. Business is really slow right now and I feel like taking a little cruise, so how about if you two just ride along for free. We just might see something interesting? I don't usually allow dogs on the boat but, since that appears to be a pretty special friend of yours, she can come along too. By the way, may name is Captain Bill." The girls introduced themselves and Maxie and they all climbed on the glass bottom boat and were soon heading out of the harbor.

Captain Bill

Once clear of the harbor they began to slowly motor just a hundred feet or so off the jagged rocks of the islands shoreline. The water dropped off real fast here, going almost straight down to the sandy bottom nearly one hundred feet below. Darting in and out of the rock formations and weaving through the towering strands of kelp that disappeared into the depths, they could see many varieties and sizes of colorful fish. Bright orange Garibaldi splashed across the scene. Over the deeper water could be seen the long slender iridescent bodies of Barracuda, gliding patiently as they waited for smaller fish to make a fatal mistake and wander too far from the protection of the reef. In the rocks they saw a lobster scurry back into a small tunnel at the sound of the boat while a slimy looking Moray eel slithered just far enough out of its hole to see what was going on. The girls' hearts quickened when they spied a formation of large manta rays gracefully gliding along the bottom. About this time, Maxie decided to make her plunge. She apparently had seen something very interesting so off she went over the side. The girls stared through the glass to watch her as she paddled down towards the rocks below, trailing a long string of bubbles.

Almost out of breath, Maxie reappeared and climbed back on board. In her mouth she was carrying a big black oyster. She walked over to Kira and gently laid it at her feet. Kira said, "Why that was very thoughtful of you Maxie but I'm sorry, I'm allergic to shell fish, we should let the poor thing go." Maxie looked up at Kira, tilted her head to the side, and rolled her eyes. She then gave three sharp barks and the girls were amazed to see the oyster slowly open its shell. Inside the oyster was a radiant pearl which Maxie gently extracted and placed in Kira's hand. Kira said, "Oh thank you Maxie, it's beautiful!" The oyster closed back up and Maxie gently picked it up and was over the side only to return in a minute with another one. The routine was repeated with Macy this time and prompted squeals of delight when Maxie placed a second pearl in her outstretched hand. Back over the side went Maxie to return the second oyster to its home.

On her way back from returning the second oyster, Maxie swam up to the glass and smiled in at the girls. But the girls weren't smiling back. They were frantically waving in an attempt to tell Maxie to get back in the boat because far below they saw the dreaded Draco swimming silently upward towards their little friend. Maxie didn't seem to notice their signals and just continued to stare in at them with that little smile on her face. But, as it turned out, Maxie had been watching Draco in the reflection off the bottom of the glass bottom boat and knew exactly what the big dummy was up to. Maxie was just waiting to make her move. In a great final thrust of speed, Draco lunged at Maxie but was totally shocked when, at the last possible moment, Maxie slipped straight sideways, clear of his snapping jaws. Unable to slow, Draco smashed headfirst right into the glass, just inches from the terrified girls. The thick glass was very strong and easily held against Draco's mighty onslaught but the same couldn't be said for Draco's snout. It looked like a crushed aluminum can. The injured shark started swimming wildly in circles in obvious pain as well as anger at being outwitted again. Meanwhile, Maxie had scampered back onto the boat and quickly ran down beside the girls just in time to stick her tongue out at Draco who had stopped circling long enough to glare at them through the glass. "That was the best!!" Maxie shouted.

Captain Bill had been up in the wheelhouse steering the boat so hadn't seen all the action going on below. He shouted down at the girls, "It's time to head back into the harbor. I sure hope you enjoyed our little cruise." "It was wonderful!" shouted Macy. "Yes it was" agreed Kira. "Thank you so much for your kindness Captain Bill". Soon they were back at the pier and said their goodbyes to Captain Bill.

Walking south out of Avalon they came upon a rocky point jutting into the ocean. They climbed onto the point and stood on a ledge high above the water. Maxie joined them and, facing the east, let out a string of high pitched yelps. Soon there were high pitched dolphin squeals in return and looking down, Kira and Macy could see their three new friends. Dolly shouted up at the girls, "We can't climb those rocks, so you girls are going to have to jump". "It's too high", said Kira. "Yah, way too high" echoed Macy. They turned to see what Maxie thought just in time to see her leap from the rocks with a loud "Geronimo". They looked at each other, grasped hands, and said softly, "Geronimo, I think" and off they went. The water was cool and refreshing and they were both giggling when they bobbed to the surface. They each climbed aboard their dolphin and were soon racing eastward towards Laguna Beach as the sun began to set over Catalina Island.

It was getting late in the day when they arrived back at Laguna and they knew that Nana and Papa Ed would be worried sick about them so they quickly thanked Dolly and her friends for all their help and bid them farewell. Dolly swam out into the waves and dove deep. To their delight, she and her two friends burst straight up from the water a moment later. Dolly did a perfect flip, landing head first, while, at the same time, her friends spun around and around and fell back into the water on their tails. "Better than Sea World" said Kira. "Way better" agreed Macy. Maxie barked in agreement and then led them over to the tunnel that led back up to the secret place.

Maxie then paused, faced the girls and spoke seriously. "I need to tell you about the rules that govern my adventures so that maybe someday I can take you on another one. First, to start an adventure, we must all join hands and say the magic chant three times "Fumbalar-Mondo-Tintular-Condol". Maxie asked the girls to repeat the chant until they got it right and then explained, "The chant won't work every time because all the planets must be in precise alignment but, when they are, and when the chant is spoken correctly, we can join in an adventure. The second rule is that, you can only tell someone about our adventure by sharing a dream with them. If you tell anyone directly, then you will instantly forget all about the adventure and we'll never be able to join on another one. Do you girls understand and can you agree to these two rules?" Kira and Macy nodded solemnly and vowed to play by the rules.

Macy said "Maxie we're way too tired to climb all the way back up to the secret place in this tunnel" Maxie said "Trust me" and headed into the tunnel. They looked at each other and Macy said, "Well everything has worked out so far so we may as well go for it." and in they went. The very instant they passed the entrance to the tunnel, they came rolling out into the secret place. Maxie had already bolted out the entrance and was barking as she ran back up the trail to Moulton Meadows. The girls followed quickly and immediately noticed that it seemed a lot brighter than it had been down at the beach. They hoped that, by some miracle, Nana and Papa Ed would be waiting for them by the picnic table.

They ran like mad back up the wilderness trail. When they got to the picnic table Nana said "lunch is almost ready but first you have to wipe off your hands with these sanitary wipes". She always made sure they cleaned up before eating. They looked at each other in surprise and Kira said, "Nana, I'm sorry we took so long, we were down at the secret place and lost track of the time". "Oh, you're not late at all." said Nana. I'm sure you were gone for less than 10 minutes but thanks for being so courteous." The girls took Maxie aside and asked her what was going on, but it seemed like Maxie hadn't been able to talk with them since they came out of the tunnel.

They enjoyed a nice lunch then. Nana had prepared servings of macaroni salad along with thick turkey sandwiches, and, of course, there were plenty of fruits and vegetables as well as chilled drinks. Nana said, "Girls, I think you were starving. If I didn't know any better, I would say you've missed a few meals." The girls both agreed as they refilled their plates. Meanwhile, Maxie was staring at Papa Ed and hoping for a handout. Like usual, Papa Ed sneaked her a few pieces of turkey, when Nana wasn't looking.

Later that night, after a tasty dinner and a long bath in Nana's Jacuzzi tub, Kira and Macy were stretched out on the guestroom bed. As always, Maxie had come in to spend the night with them. Macy said "Sissy did we really go to Catalina today and have an adventure or was I just dreaming. How could all of that happen in just 10 minutes?" Kira said, "I don't know. We must have somehow had the same dream. Maybe that can happen sometimes with sisters who love each other as much as we do. It was a great dream though wasn't it?" "Yes it sure was said Macy."

Just then, Maxie gave a little bark and went to get Macy's shorts that were hanging over the chair. She hopped up on the bed and dropped them on Macy's lap. Macy exclaimed, "What are you doing Maxie? Yuk, these shorts are all dirty!" Not to be deterred, Maxie nudged Macy's hand to the pocket of the shorts and when Macy reached in she felt a small round object and pulled it out to see what it was. When she opened her hand she was stunned! It was a beautiful pearl. "Wow!" screamed Macy, "look at this!" Kira flew out of the bed and grabbed her shorts and, sure enough, deep inside the pocket she found her pearl and then it was her turn to scream in delight. "You girls settle down now and go to sleep", came Nana's voice from down the hall. Giggling delightedly, the girls gave each other a big hug and then hugged Maxie between them. Kira said "Thanks for the wonderful adventure Maxie. I love you." "Me to", said Macy.

With their pearls safely hidden away, the girls were soon fast asleep. Maxie stayed awake for awhile thinking about what other adventures lay ahead. She had overheard Nana excitedly telling Papa Ed that Evan and Grayson would be visiting them back in Minnesota the coming summer so perhaps she would invite the two boys to share an adventure with her there. She would give that more thought. But soon, Maxie was fast asleep and drifted into a great dream about dodging Draco and finally catching Polly.

It was a few weeks later that Nana and Papa Ed received a wonderful surprise gift from Kira and Macy. Together they had painted a truly amazing scene with Kira doing the drawing and Macy the coloring. It depicted three dolphins skimming the waves toward what looked like a distant island and there was a big pelican flying out ahead of them. A little black dog was standing on the lead dolphin and its ears were stuck straight out in the wind. It looked like it had one paw up and was pointing in the direction of the island. Just behind, astride the other two dolphins were two young girls. Their hair was blowing straight back and their arms were straight out beside them as their legs gripped their galloping dolphins. Upon seeing the painting, Papa Ed and Nana were delighted. Nana said, "This is so beautiful, we must frame it and hang it in a place of honor". Papa Ed agreed and went on to say, "Those girls sure have vivid imaginations! Who would ever think of riding dolphins like that? It's really crazy but it's kind of cute isn't it?" "Yes" agreed Nana. "I wonder how they dream those things up."

THE END

Printed in the United States
By Bookmasters